GH01033098

CONTENTS

Prayers   2

Psalms and Other Scriptural Songs   15

Readings from the Bible   21

Prayers

Our Father, who art in heaven,
   hallowed be thy Name,
   thy kingdom come,
   thy will be done,
      on earth as it is in heaven.
Give us this day our daily bread.
And forgive us our trespasses,
   as we forgive those
      who trespass against us.
And lead us not into temptation,
   but deliver us from evil.
For thine is the kingdom,
   and the power, and the glory,
   for ever and ever. Amen.

or

Our Father in heaven,
   hallowed be your Name,
   your kingdom come,
   your will be done,
      on earth as in heaven.
Give us today our daily bread.
Forgive us our sins
   as we forgive those
      who sin against us.
Save us from the time of trial,
   and deliver us from evil.
For the kingdom, the power,
   and the glory are yours,
      now and for ever. Amen.

FOR TRUST IN GOD

O God, the source of all health: So fill
my heart with faith in your love, that
with calm expectancy I may make room
for your power to possess me, and grace-
fully accept your healing; through Jesus
Christ our Lord. Amen.

or this

God of all comfort, our very present help
in trouble, be near to me. Look on me
with the eyes of your mercy; comfort me
with a sense of your presence; preserve

3

me from the enemy; and give me patience in my affliction. Restore me to health, and lead me to your eternal glory; through Jesus Christ our Lord. Amen.

IN PAIN

Lord Jesus Christ, by your patience in suffering you hallowed earthly pain and gave us the example of obedience to your Father's will: Be near me in my time of weakness and pain; sustain me by your grace, that my strength and courage may not fail; heal me according to your will; and help me always to believe that what happens to me here is of little account if you hold me in eternal life, my Lord and my God. Amen.

or this

As Jesus cried out on the cross, I cry out to you in pain, O God my Creator. Do not forsake me. Grant me relief from this suffering and preserve me in peace; through Jesus Christ my Savior, in the power of the Holy Spirit. Amen.

FOR SLEEP

O heavenly Father, you give your children

sleep for the refreshing of soul and body:
Grant me this gift, I pray; keep me in
that perfect peace which you have promised to those whose minds are fixed on
you; and give me such a sense of your
presence, that in the hours of silence I
may enjoy the blessed assurance of your
love; through Jesus Christ our Savior.
Amen.

or this

Holy and Blessed One: shine on me as I
lie sleepless. Illumine my spirit and give
me rest in you, so that I may recognize
you as the true God who brings us out of
darkness into your eternal light. Amen.

IN THE MORNING

This is another day, O Lord. I know not
what it will bring forth, but make me
ready, Lord, for whatever it may be. If I
am to stand up, help me to stand bravely.
If I am to sit still, help me to sit quietly.
If I am to lie low, help me to do it
patiently. And if I am to do nothing, let
me do it gallantly. Make these words
more than words, and give me the Spirit
of Jesus. Amen.

or this

Lord God, almighty and everlasting
Father, you have brought me in safety to
this new day: Preserve me with your
mighty power, that I may not fall into
sin, nor be overcome by adversity; and in
all I do, direct me to the fulfilling of your
purpose; through Jesus Christ our Lord.
Amen.

IN THE EVENING

Lord Jesus, stay with me, for evening is at
hand and the day is past; be my companion in the way, kindle my heart, and
awaken my hope, that I may know you as
you are revealed in Scripture and the
breaking of bread. Grant this for the sake
of your love. Amen.

FOR PROTECTION

Christ, light of light, brightness inde-
scribable, the Wisdom, power and glory
of God, the Word made flesh: you over-
came the forces of Satan, redeemed the
world, then ascended again to the Father.
Grant me, I pray, in this tarnished world,
the shining of your splendor. Send your

Archangel Michael to defend me, to guard my going out and coming in, and to bring me safely to your presence, where you reign in the one holy and undivided Trinity, to ages of ages. Amen.

IN TIMES OF MENTAL DISTRESS

Blessed Jesus, in the comfort of your love, I lay before you the memories that haunt me, the anxieties that perplex me, the despair that frightens me, and my frustration at my inability to think clearly. Help me to discover your forgiveness in my memories and know your peace in my distress. Touch me, O Lord, and fill me with your light and your hope. Amen.

FOR RECOVERY FROM SICKNESS

Spirit of all healing, visit me, your child; in your power, renew health within me and raise me up in joy, according to your loving-kindness, for which I give thanks and praise; through Jesus Christ our Savior. Amen.

FOR STRENGTH AND CONFIDENCE

Gracious God, only source of life and

health: Help, comfort, and relieve me, and give your power of healing to those who minister to my needs; that my weakness may be turned to strength and confidence in your loving care; for the sake of Jesus Christ. Amen.

FOR GUIDANCE

Heavenly Father, in you I live and move and have my being: I humbly pray you so to guide and govern me by your Holy Spirit, that in all the cares and occupations of this life I may not forget you, but may remember that I am ever walking in your sight; through Jesus Christ our Lord. Amen.

FOR REST

O God my refuge and strength: in this place of unrelenting light and noise, enfold me in your holy darkness and silence, that I may rest secure under the shadow of your wings. Amen.

FOR SANCTIFICATION OF ILLNESS

Sanctify, O Holy One, my sickness, that awareness of weakness may add strength to my faith and determination to my repentance; and grant that I may be made whole, according to your will; through Jesus Christ our Savior. Amen.

BEFORE AN OPERATION

Loving God, I pray that you will comfort me in my suffering, lend skill to the hands of my healers, and bless the means used for my cure. Give me such confidence in the power of your grace, that even when I am afraid, I may put my whole trust in you; through our Savior Jesus Christ. Amen.

FOR AN EXTENDED COURSE OF TREATMENT

Strengthen me, O God, to go where I have to go and bear what I have to bear; that, accepting your healing gifts at the hands of surgeons, nurses, and technicians, I may be restored to wholeness with a thankful heart; through Jesus Christ our Savior. Amen.

FOR A SURVIVOR OF ABUSE AND VIOLENCE

Holy One, you do not distance yourself from the pain of your people, but in Jesus bear that pain with us and bless all who suffer at others' hands. Hallow my flesh and all creation; with your cleansing love bring me healing and strength; and by your justice, lift me up, that in the body you have given me, I may again rejoice. In Jesus' name I pray. Amen.

IN TIMES OF PERSONAL DISTRESS

Lord Christ, you came into the world as one of us, and suffered as we do. As I go through the trials of life, help me to realize that you are with me at all times and in all things; that I have no secrets from you; and that your loving grace enfolds me for eternity. In the security of your embrace I pray. Amen.

THANKSGIVING FOR RECOVERY

God, your loving-kindness never fails and your mercies are new every morning. I thank you for giving me relief from pain and hope of health renewed. Continue the good work begun in me; that increasing daily in wholeness and strength, I may rejoice in your goodness and so order my life always to think and do that which pleases you; through Jesus Christ our Redeemer. Amen.

FOR ONE WHO FEARS LOSING HOPE

Loving God, by your Holy Spirit inspire me, as I fear losing hope. Give me a fresh vision of your love, that I may find again what I fear I have lost. Grant me your powerful deliverance; through the One who makes all things new, Jesus Christ our Redeemer. Amen.

IN THANKSGIVING

In the midst of illness, God, I pause to give you thanks: for the glory of creation, which reveals in many forms your matchless beauty; for the life, death, and resurrection of Jesus our Savior; for your gift of my life and the presence of the Holy Spirit; for loved ones who care for me; and for the companionship of the Church. I thank you, blessed Trinity, holy God, for the gifts which sustain me in my time of need. Amen.

IN LOSS OF MEMORY

Holy God, you have known me from my mother's womb, and have been with me throughout my life. Protect me and keep me safe through all the changes that may

come. Since I am sealed as Christ's own,
help me to trust that who I am will never
be lost to you. Amen.

IN CONFINEMENT

My Creator, you rolled out the heavens
and spread the sky like a tent: bless to
me the small confinement of this room,
the long days, disturbances of night,
immobility of body, and unease of soul,
that this place of exile may become my
holy ground, and Jesus my deliverer.
Amen.

FOR SERENITY

Merciful Jesus, you are my guide, the joy
of my heart, the author of my hope, and
the object of my love. I come seeking
refreshment and peace. Show me your
mercy, relieve my fears and anxieties, and
grant me a quiet mind and an expectant
heart, that by the assurance of your
presence I may learn to abide in you,
my Lord and my God. Amen.

or this

Jesus, let your mighty calmness lift me
above my fears and frustrations. By your

deep patience, give me tranquility and
stillness of soul in you. Make me in this,
and in all, more and more like you.
Amen.

A PRAYER OF THANKSGIVING FOR CAREGIVERS

Merciful God, I thank you that since I
have no strength to care for myself, you
serve me through the hands and hearts of
others. Bless these people that they may
continue to serve you and please you all
their days. Amen.

A PRAYER OF COMFORT IN GOD

God, you are my help and comfort; you
shelter and surround me in love so tender
that I may know your presence with me,
now and always. Amen.

IN DESOLATION

O God, why have you abandoned me?
Though you have hidden your face from
me, still from this dread and empty place,
I cry to you, who have promised me that
underneath are your everlasting arms.
Amen.

AFTER THE LOSS OF A PREGNANCY

O God, who gathered Rachel's tears over her lost children, hear now my/our sorrow and distress at the death of my/our expected child; in the darkness of loss, stretch out to me/us the strength of your arm and renewed assurance of your love; through your own suffering and risen Child Jesus. Amen.

FOR DIAGNOSIS OF TERMINAL ILLNESS

O God, only you number my days. Help me to look bravely at the end of my life in this world, while trusting in my life in the next. Journey with me toward my unexplored horizon where Jesus my Savior has gone before. Amen.

FOR DIFFICULT TREATMENT CHOICES

Jesus, at Gethsemane you toiled with terrifying choices. Be with me now as I struggle with a fearful choice of treatments which promise much discomfort and offer no guarantee of long-term good. Help me know that you will bless my choice to me, and, good Savior, be my companion on the way. Amen.

Psalms and
Other Scriptural Songs

O God, you are my shepherd;
   I shall not be in want.
You make me lie down in green pastures
   and lead me beside still waters.
You revive my soul
   and guide me along right pathways
   for the sake of your Name.
Though I walk through the valley of the
     shadow of death,
I shall fear no evil,
   for you are with me;
   your rod and your staff, they comfort me.
You spread a table before me in the
     presence of those who trouble me;
   you have anointed my head with oil,
   and my cup is running over.
Surely your goodness and mercy shall
     follow me all the days of my life,
   and I will dwell in the house of God
     for ever.
—*Psalm 23*

IN TIMES OF DISTRESS

How long, O God?
Will you forget me for ever;
  how long will you hide your face
    from me?
How long shall I have perplexity in my
    mind
and grief in my heart, day after day;
  how long shall my enemy triumph
    over me?
Look upon me and answer me, O God,
    my God;
  give light to my eyes, lest I sleep
    in death;
Lest my enemies say they have prevailed
    over me,
  and my foes rejoice that I have fallen.
But I put my trust in your mercy;
my heart is joyful because of your saving
    help.
  I will sing to the Holy One, who has
    dealt with me richly;
  I will praise the Name of God Most
    High.
—*Psalm 13*

IN TIMES OF LONELINESS

To you, O God, I lift up my soul;
my God, I put my trust in you;
   let me not be humiliated,
      nor let my enemies triumph over me.
Turn to me and have pity on me,
   for I am left alone and in misery.
The sorrows of my heart have increased;
   bring me out of my troubles.
Look upon my adversity and misery,
   and forgive me all my sin.
Protect my life and deliver me;
   let me not be put to shame, for I
      have trusted in you.
Let integrity and uprightness preserve me,
   for my hope has been in you.
–Psalm 25:1, 15-17, 19-20

FOR STRENGTH

Bless the Lord, O my soul,
   and all that is within me, bless his
      holy Name.
Bless the Lord, O my soul,
   and forget not all his benefits.
He forgives all your sins
   and heals all your infirmities.
—Psalm 103:1-3

THE SAVING POWER OF GOD

Surely, it is God who saves me;
   I will trust in him and not be afraid.
For the Lord is my stronghold and my
     sure defense,
   and he will be my Savior.
Therefore you shall draw water with
     rejoicing
   from the springs of salvation.
And on that day you shall say,
   Give thanks to the Lord and call
     upon his Name;
Make his deeds known among the peoples;
   see that they remember that his
     Name is exalted.
Sing the praises of the Lord, for he has
     done great things,
   and this is known in all the world.
Cry aloud, inhabitants of Zion, ring out
     your joy,
   for the great one in the midst of you
     is the Holy One of Israel.
—*Isaiah 12:2-6*

A SONG OF THANKSGIVING

I will exalt you, O holy God,
   and bless your Name for ever and ever.

Every day will I bless you
    and praise your Name for ever and ever.
Great are you, O God, and greatly to be
        praised;
    there is no end to your greatness.
One generation shall praise your works to
        another
    and shall declare your power.
I will ponder the glorious splendor of
        your majesty
    and all your marvelous works.
They shall speak of the might of your
        wondrous acts,
    and I will tell of your greatness.
They shall publish the remembrance of
        your great goodness;
    they shall sing of your righteous deeds.
You are gracious and full of compassion,
    slow to anger and of great kindness.
You are loving to everyone,
    and your compassion is over all your
        works.
All your works praise you, O God,
    and your faithful servants bless you.
They make known the glory of your realm
    and speak of your power,
That the peoples may know of your power

and the glorious splendor of your
dominion.
Yours, O God, is an everlasting reign;
your dominion endures throughout
all ages.
—*Psalm 145:1-4, 8-13*

THE SONG OF MARY

My soul proclaims the greatness
of the Lord,
my spirit rejoices in you, O God my
Savior,
for you have looked with favor on
your lowly servant.
From this day all generations will
call me blessed:
you, the Almighty, have done great
things for me,
and holy is your Name.
You have mercy on those who fear you
from generation to generation.
You have shown strength with your arm
and scattered the proud in their
conceit,
Casting down the mighty from their
thrones
and lifting up the lowly.

You have filled the hungry with good things
    and sent the rich away empty.
You have come to the help of your
        servant Israel,
    for you have remembered your
        promise of mercy,
The promise made to our forebears,
    to Abraham and his children for ever.
—*Luke 1:46-55*

Readings from the Bible

GOD'S POWERFUL PRESENCE
I, the Lord your God, hold your right
hand: it is I who say to you, "Do not fear,
I will help you." —*Isaiah 41:13*

GOD'S CONSOLING GRACE
Blessed be the God and Father of our
Lord Jesus Christ, the Father of mercies
and the God of all consolation, who con-
soles us in all our affliction, so that we
may be able to console those who are in
any affliction with the consolation with
which we ourselves are consoled by God.
For just as the sufferings of Christ are

abundant for us, so also our consolation
is abundant through Christ.
—*2 Corinthians 1:3-5*

IN TIMES OF WEARINESS
AND FATIGUE

Jesus said, "Come to me, all you that are
weary and are carrying heavy burdens,
and I will give you rest. Take my yoke
upon you, and learn from me; for I am
gentle and humble in heart, and you will
find rest for your souls. For my yoke is
easy, and my burden is light."
—*Matthew 11:28-30*

IN TIMES OF GREAT DISTRESS—
THE COURAGE OF JESUS

They went to a place called Gethsemane;
and Jesus said to his disciples, "Sit here
while I pray." He took with him Peter
and James and John, and began to be dis-
tressed and agitated. And he said to
them, "I am deeply grieved, even to
death; remain here, and keep awake."
And going a little farther, he threw himself on the ground and prayed that, if it
were possible, the hour might pass from
him. He said, "Abba, Father, for you all

things are possible; remove this cup from me; yet, not what I want, but what you want." —*Mark 14:32-36*

JESUS OUR NOURISHMENT

Jesus said, "Very truly, I tell you, whoever believes has eternal life. I am the bread of life. Your ancestors ate the manna in the wilderness, and they died. This is the bread that comes down from heaven, so that one may eat of it and not die. I am the living bread that came down from heaven. Whoever eats of this bread will live for ever; and the bread that I will give for the life of the world is my flesh. Those who eat my flesh and drink my blood have eternal life, and I will raise them up on the last day; for my flesh is true food and my blood is true drink." —*John 7:47-51, 54-55*

GOD OUR PROTECTOR

Because you are bound to me in love, therefore will I deliver you; I will protect you, because you know my Name. You shall call upon me, and I will answer you; I am with you in trouble; I will rescue you and bring you honor. —*Psalm 91:14-15*

THE POWER OF PRAYER

I write these things to you who believe in
the name of the Son of God, so that you
may know that you have eternal life.
And this is the boldness we have in him,
that if we ask anything according to his
will, he hears us. And if we know that he
hears us in whatever we ask, we know
that we have obtained the requests made
of him. —*1 John 5:13-15*

IN TIMES OF WORRY

Cast all your anxiety on God, because he
cares for you. —*1 Peter 5:7*

GOD'S ABIDING FAITHFULNESS

May the God of peace himself sanctify
you entirely; and may your spirit and soul
and body be kept sound and blameless at
the coming of our Lord Jesus Christ. The
one who calls you is faithful, and he will
do this. —*1 Thessalonians 5:23-24*

THE ENDURING POWER
OF GOD'S LOVE

If God is for us, who is against us? He
who did not withhold his own Son, but
gave him up for all of us, will he not with